Haiku and Hope

Haiku and Hope
50 States of Climate Change

Maggie Dewane

Fulcrum Publishing
Lakewood, Colorado

Library of Congress Cataloging-in-Publication Data
Names: Dewane, Maggie, author.
Title: Haikus and hope : 50 states of climate change / Maggie Dewane.
Description: Lakewood, CO : Fulcrum Publishing, 2025. | Series: Eco
poetry
Identifiers: LCCN 2024034408 (print) | LCCN 2024034409 (ebook) | ISBN
   9781682754962 (trade paperback) | ISBN 9781682754979 (ebook)
Subjects: LCSH: Climatic changes--United States--States--Poetry. | U.S.
   states--Environmental conditions--Poetry. | Haiku, American.
Classification: LCC PS595.C554 D49 2025 (print) | LCC PS595.C554
(ebook)
   | DDC 811/.6--dc23/eng/20250131
LC record available at https://lccn.loc.gov/2024034408
LC ebook record available at https://lccn.loc.gov/2024034409

Printed in the United States
0 9 8 7 6 5 4 3 2 1

Cover Illustration and Design by Kateri Kramer

Fulcrum Publishing
7333 W. Jefferson Ave., Suite 225
Lakewood, CO 80235
(800) 992-2908 • (303) 277-1623
www.fulcrumbooks.com

For Mr. Davis and Mr. Labecki
and the teachers who empower their students.

And of course, for Argos.

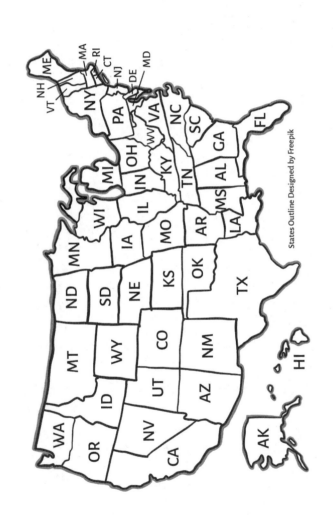

States Outline Designed by Freepik

Contents

STATES BY ANOTHER NAME

Initiation

"South Dakota?" I asked. "Why would we go there?" As a naïve 25-year-old, I assumed there was nothing worth seeing out there. But my then-boyfriend convinced me we'd go, we'd hike, and we'd enjoy it. We had just finished graduate school, and I was itching to reenter the work world—it had been a year since I left my job in the U.S. Senate and I was filled with self-importance, thinking no time should ever be wasted. But we found ourselves jobless and unlikely to ever have this "funemployment" freedom again. So despite my protests, we set out on a two-month cross-country road trip camping, hiking, crashing on friends' couches, stumbling into towns we'd never heard of, and discovering the quality and charisma of the United States.

That trip spurred an appreciation in me for the uniqueness of our country. I'd grown up in suburban Pennsylvania, the daughter of public servants, one a tree-hugging social worker. At an early age, I learned that representation matters, that the government has a duty to support its people, and that we share this planet with more than just humans. But it's one thing to intellectually know these concepts, and it's another to experience them. We can read books, watch the news, and listen to podcasts—that feeds our brains. But to feed our minds and souls, we must open ourselves to the world outside of what is comfortable, and that often means seizing opportunity and putting ourselves into new situations. My 27-state adventure in 2013 exposed me to varied and remarkable perspectives and stories that exist everywhere, not just in the fabled landscapes of wanderlust adventures.

In the years since, I have crisscrossed the country visiting all 50 states, often solo or with my 100-lb. furry mountain dog, Argos, by my side. While I've had my fair share of grungy motels, speeding tickets, and questionable choices, I can't get enough of the thrill that is leaving home to see what else is out there. My parents call it the "travel bug," but I prefer to give the urge a purpose—however lofty—and think of it as a quest to know the unknown. I prefer to imagine that my ancestors were explorers, and that my modern-day thirst for discovery has been passed down like a precious heirloom.

Driving this insatiable curiosity is the underlying current of sanctuary in nature. It's there that I'm most alive—finding gratitude in every quiet step on pine needle–laden trails, seeking the wisdom of ancient trees and groaning glaciers, and gaining strength from the purity of wild creatures. Nature is poetry: words suspended together that can evoke explicit meaning or leave space for interpretation, imagination, and revelation.

Poetry is subjective; the reader has the power to absorb words on a page in whatever way resonates with them. Of course, the poet may intend a certain message, but just as oil on canvas can be enjoyed in an infinite number of ways, so too can poetry. Plenty of people are put off by poetry, claiming it's intimidating, esoteric, or just plain weird. I'm the first to admit it *can* be those things, but it is also wonderfully inclusive, much like music. We've all sung along to songs of heartbreak, thinking the tragedy aligns so perfectly with our own aches that the songwriter must surely have had the exact same experience. But that doesn't have to be true, because every person's life experience is different. Therein is the magic of words. They put names to our emotions—they capture meaning and connect us, creating relatability and trust.

I've been writing poetry since middle school, trying to put my finger on feelings, think in ways that haven't been thought, or create snapshots of worlds I visit in my dreams. For me, it's a less direct, more intriguing way of saying "I'm angry," or "This crazy thing happened to me." It gives me permission to be creative, embellish— and *explore*. Poetry offers the opportunity to explore ideas and emotions, uncover new perspectives, and be authentically ourselves because there's no right or wrong way to do it.

Inspired by my love of this country and my travels throughout it, I started writing haiku poems for all 50 states. Haiku is a Japanese style of poetry that most often follows the three-line format of five-seven-five syllables, respectively. Haiku aim to tap into our senses, typically evoking playful or tranquil images of nature. I've always enjoyed their simplicity and staying power; a good haiku can be memorized, kept in a back pocket, and enjoyed later. They can be whimsical and surprising or thoughtful and melodic. For the uninitiated, they are an accessible entry to the world of poetry.

As I wrote my haiku, I wondered what might happen when these poems—these realities—are juxtaposed with the looming dread of the climate crisis. I studied environmental science and policy in graduate school and have made my career as a climate communicator, running the press department of environmental nonprofits, contributing guest articles and interviews to news outlets on melting poles and rising seas, and filming climate impacts and conservation efforts from every continent. So to conjure imagery of a changing world, I wrote a second haiku for each U.S. state: an image of that state changed by the climate crisis.

This book's intention is to provide a picture of climate change as it's happening around our country, first through the creative lens of poetry. Part II of this book, which follows the haiku, delves into these changes and posits how and why we should preserve our home. Amid the humdrum of daily life and the onslaught of the 24/7 media cycle, it's nearly impossible to make sense of all the information thrown at us. My hope for this book is that it will lessen some of the overwhelmingness of climate change for you, because in the fight against climate change, we all need to play a role—and we cannot know our role if we don't know the fight.

I invite you to join me—find your beloved home within these pages and revel in its splendor, enchantment, and beauty. Take time to explore and contemplate scenes of places unfamiliar. And along the way, be mindful of the changes our homes are likely to see, if they are not already seeing them.

Alabama

Warm air rises in

slow, understated mornings.

Afternoon downpour.

Alabama Changed

Churning water floods

the streets—erodes our shores with

heavy humid heat.

Alaska

Sleepy glacier stands,

groans, and stretches its blue bones.

Wading moose cries out.

Alaska Changed

We have abandoned

our villages, swallowed by

ice melt; creeping seas.

Arizona

Grand rivers forge time,

earth hallowed with memory.

Eras etched in stone.

Arizona Changed

With the rivers gone,

the desert is left lonely,

desolate and scorched.

Arkansas

Deep and jagged caves

twist and turn with marked silence.

Emerge for hot springs.

Arkansas Changed

Wall of water speeds

suddenly. Unwelcome guest

during prolonged droughts.

California

Rugged yet refined.

Mountaineers earn postcards of

the greatest of trees.

California Changed

Smoke fills sky and lungs,

fires rage without prejudice.

Not enough water.

Colorado

Bold and beautiful,

blue sky sunshine meets white snow.

Swish goes that fresh pow.

Colorado Changed

Thirty, seventy—

temperatures change, can't plan.

Less snow, less flow. Dry.

Connecticut

Pockets of forest,

woodland reflections on glass.

Once new, now antique.

Connecticut Changed

Each spring comes sooner,

with pummeling rain and floods.

Extreme becomes norm.

Delaware

Evening summer breeze.

I dig my toes in the sand,

gaze out, taste freedom.

Delaware Changed

Consider the loss:

eight percent of land is gone.

We who are so small.

Florida

A smell all its own—
inhale salt, swamp, citrus, and . . .
Respect the mangroves.

Florida Changed

Hardened coastlines shrink,
engulfed by high tide daily.
When will we believe?

Georgia

Paddle through wetland,

duck under limbs, brushing leaves.

Then, *splunk!* Tiny frog.

Georgia Changed

Onslaught of impacts—

more fire and flood, rising seas;

storms and heat that kill.

Hawai'i

Underwater world:

I watch a sea turtle swim.

With her, I exist.

Hawai'i Changed

Watching the land grab

where fire meets the sea, I plea,

malama pono.

Idaho

I passed through quickly
but stopped for gold potatoes:
snacks on bright green hills.

Idaho Changed

Crop storage questions—
too warm, ruined yields. So, must
we import taters?

Illinois

> With a gust of wind
> I might forget it's summer.
> The lake's breath cools me.

Illinois Changed

> Rain. Rain. Rain. Rain. Rain.
> Stressed drainage systems collapse
> our water, our health.

Indiana

We walked many stairs
to reach the dunes and lakeshore.
New national park.

Indiana Changed

Muddy and messy
walks spent fighting off the bugs.
Just don't go outside.

Iowa

Wind kisses soft grains:

wheat blossoms stir in the breeze.

Amber horizon.

Iowa Changed

Repeated flooding,

plus deadly hot work outdoors.

Waterlogged and wrecked.

Kansas

Sunshine bursts but then
ominous clouds rumble deep.
Weather turns quick here.

Kansas Changed

Crops are livelihoods.
With less freeze, more pests, disease—
livelihoods threatened.

Kentucky

Strawberries and cream,

bourbon shared on a front porch:

warm evening moments.

Kentucky Changed

Earth vibrates under

a chaotic black sky. Homes

soon cease to exist.

Louisiana

Rhythm and soul are

everywhere. Even in food.

Flavors of the Gulf.

Louisiana Changed

Stronger hurricanes

batter all. Resilience wanes.

Many can't escape.

Maine

Walking through soft mist,
a heightened smell of spruce trails,
late spring's dewy ferns.

Maine Changed

Slush over snowshoes
and the fastest-warming seas.
Not how life should be.

Maryland

Defined by water;

reveries of history.

It's time to pick crabs.

Maryland Changed

Water that can't breathe.

Surging seas swallow cities.

Humidity hangs.

Massachusetts

Fall: golden sunshine,
orange leaves, smells of apple
on waterside walks.

Massachusetts Changed

Bugs in November,
no need for cozy sweaters—
where did winter go?

Michigan

Summer sun shower—

rain droplets speckle my tent.

Morning's fresh greeting.

Michigan Changed

Climate predictions:

bad, but perhaps less extreme.

Refuge from the change.

Minnesota

Float across the lake

lazily, watch walleye jump.

Wave to passersby.

Minnesota Changed

Heat waves blast, sizzle,

Arctic air freezes, cripples.

Outside is deadly.

Mississippi

Damp dirt underfoot,

cacophony of insects,

Black moss overhead.

Mississippi Changed

Wildfire surprises

our state; never thought of them.

Floods don't remedy.

Missouri

Winding backroads tempt
me to keep on exploring.
Bats dancing at dusk.

Missouri Changed

Up goes heat index,
up goes precipitation,
down goes public health.

Montana

Everything wild, plus

belt buckles, boots, ranch and range.

A fearless frontier.

Montana Changed

Lungs gasp, constricted

by air once perfectly clear.

Brittle grass crunches.

Nebraska

Sunset on the hill,

laughter shared between strangers:

sweet gift of summer.

Nebraska Changed

Rains when it shouldn't.

Sun blisters when it shouldn't.

Weather is confused.

Nevada

Sinking in vastness,
my eyes fill with endless sand;
find the oasis.

Nevada Changed

Hotter already:
lake levels plummeting fast,
barrenness coming.

New Hampshire

Snow crunches, crisp air,

small towns of worn jeans and plaid.

Resolute outdoors.

New Hampshire Changed

Warm temperatures;

losing our identity.

Mountains melt away.

New Jersey

Meadowlands metal
from north to south, diverse we.
Pinelands of soft green.

New Jersey Changed

The Shore wears down and
creeping beachfront property
succumbs to the sea.

New Mexico

Pinyon jay and pine

subtly ripple through cultures;

Earth mother provides.

New Mexico Changed

More snow, but more drought.

Pendulum swings the seasons.

Unquenched thirst of earth.

New York

She's a state of mind:

embrace it all, arms outstretched.

Gorges to Gotham.

New York Changed

Forests grow warmer,

subways are underwater.

No one is immune.

North Carolina

I breathe sticky air,

jump into lakeside relief.

Alas, mosquitoes.

North Carolina Changed

Faces lose color—

we can't afford to cool down.

Exhausted by heat.

North Dakota

Lightning streaks the sky
over prairie's rumbling hooves.
Onward to the storm.

North Dakota Changed

Elders see the change:
When the snow melts, it's summer.
Gone are fall and spring.

Ohio

Acorns and buckeyes.
Autumn—in its sweet grandeur—
letting the past go.

Ohio Changed

Heat waves in autumn
increase stress on farmers who
will lose more than crops.

Oklahoma

I await alone,

standing on the windy plain,

for the rains to come.

Oklahoma Changed

It's getting hotter:

a parched landscape, killer heat.

The sun weighs us down.

Oregon

Hush, feel the Earth's breath.

Alone with my forest kin,

it is—I am—safe.

Oregon Changed

Smoke and wind bring fire.

No alarm—we must be safe.

Wrong. Home and dog gone.

Pennsylvania

Napping in the grass,

in the green hues of summer:

sleepy adventure.

Pennsylvania Changed

Less winter snowfall

means we're shedding heavy coats.

Clammy December.

Rhode Island

Shorebirds flirt with waves;
I watch them as I skip stones.
Shared lives by the sea.

Rhode Island Changed

Precipitation.
Crash, splash rages the ocean.
Seawalls, not enough.

South Carolina

Warm sandy sunrise,

turtles crawl across the shore.

Make way—let them through!

South Carolina Changed

Hot sandless beachfront

from rising seas, erosion.

Turtles get lost, roast.

South Dakota

Scrambling amongst rocks,
new terrain round every bend:
Prairie dogs stand, chirp.

South Dakota Changed

Invasive species,
fire, and flood: bad goes the land.
No buffalo roam.

Tennessee

Here the hills have heart—
listen closely for their tune.
Come here, dance with me.

Tennessee Changed

More rushing rivers.
Pummeled by storms, rising temps,
the hills disappear.

Texas

Heavy sun and dust,

stone walkways embracing shade,

people of warm grit.

Texas Changed

Hotter and dryer—

but what are these winter storms?

We are not prepared.

Utah

Life elevated:

deep reds, sand flats, clear winters.

Here, my heart is home.

Utah Changed

Sizzling pavement,

cracking skin, nothing to drink.

No relief at night.

Vermont

Verdant and vibrant,

forest magic speaks to me.

I'm here, listening.

Vermont Changed

No more winter sports.

No more puffer and beanie.

No more white Christmas.

Virginia

Flock to forests, to
mountains older than ancient.
Escape the cities.

Virginia Changed

November nineteenth:
it's too hot in the mountains.
Winter is smaller.

Washington

Cool air blankets my

bare arms as I hike mountains.

Evergreen towers.

Washington Changed

Wish you'd have known them:

orcas, grizzlies, and barred owls.

Now barren, empty.

West Virginia

Broccoli-like trees

Winding through the wild slowly

Look up, deep valley.

West Virginia Changed

Waters rise, trapped, while

bridges fail and roads sink. Still:

"Let coal continue."

Wisconsin

Soak in Devil's Lake,

"Hello!" to hikers and dogs—

friends among strangers.

Wisconsin Changed

Indiscriminate,

thieving extreme heat steals lives.

We're losing ourselves.

Wyoming

A deep wilderness:
freedom is open terrain.
Stop. Hear the thunder.

Wyoming Changed

Lower flows, less fish.
We're downstream and feel the strain
of scarce resources.

States by Another Name

Though Washington D.C. and Puerto Rico have not been afforded statehood (and the benefits that come with it), their identities help comprise the United States as much as the other 50. These two territories, along with four others in the Atlantic and Pacific Oceans (U.S. Virgin Islands, American Samoa, Guam, and Northern Mariana Islands) are home to tax-paying U.S. citizens, but have nonvoting representation in the U.S. House of Representatives. Washington D.C. and Puerto Rico have for years called out this unfair taxation without representation, urging and advocating for statehood.

Washington D.C.

Center of the world,

where rocks, creeks, and rivers keep

pace: move and go-go.

Washington D.C. Changed

Higher tides, flash floods.

Her heart shrivels in the heat—

climate injustice.

Puerto Rico

Bomba es nuestro
Guitar strumming in the hills,
we danced in the night.

Puerto Rico Changed

Swallowed by the sea.
Who will come to our rescue?
The future is now.

Notes

Hawai'i: *Malama pono* is Hawaiian for "take good care" and often implies to take care of oneself, others, and the earth.

Puerto Rico: *Bomba* refers to a variety of vibrant musical styles and dances in Puerto Rico. This phrase is translated as *We are bomba*.

Reflection, Projection

Heavy snow falls outside my window. It's late January and the first time Washington D.C. has seen snow this winter. An unabashed lover of the cold and snow, I long for days like this—for fresh powder, spontaneous snowball fights, and chunky knit sweaters with a hot toddy. But they have become less frequent, and across the country, it's been a remarkably dry season.

Weather patterns have been shifting since the 1970s, coinciding with scientists' first revelation that industrialization could alter the way our planet behaves. The way you and I experience a day outside is weather. String a lot of weather together seasonally over time, and you get weather patterns, or climate. When those patterns change and repeatedly trend toward a new set of patterns year after year, life as we know it will also shift. This is climate change.

As Meredith Hooper describes in her book *The Ferocious Summer*, climate change is not a blanket distributed evenly across the planet. It affects regions differently simply because weather and climate are different across the planet. Jet streams and ocean currents deliver the weather patterns that create the normal humidity in Houston, blizzards in Buffalo, and tornadoes in Topeka. Climate change pushes those jet streams out of their norms so we see ice

storms in Dallas, heat waves in Portland, and prolonged drought
in Sarasota. Climate change is happening due to the planet getting
hotter, and that's known as global warming. Global warming is linked
directly to the increased burning of fossil fuels that power consumer
choices across the globe. So while Minnesota might now experience a
bomb cyclone of Arctic proportions, the frigid temperatures are
ultimately tied to a shift in the region's weather patterns as caused by
an increasing global average temperature. Today we stand teetering
on the edge of climate catastrophe. The cost of inaction is a dangerous
alteration of life as we know it: mass extinction of species, billions of
taxpayer dollars stretched across environmental disaster relief, public
health consequences that shift health baselines and increase early
mortality, decreased food and water availability followed by increased
prices for both. The list goes on.

I'm brought back to the gentle snow outside my window, cre-
ating the stuff of postcards on the window ledge and trees outside.
I think of the bustling city outside my door, dictating policy for the
people. Then I think of "we, the people," and how we deserve better
out of the officials we elect. We need leaders with forethought,
who understand the impacts of inaction and aren't consumed by
greed and the deep pockets of special interest groups that buy their
loyalty. This need isn't unique to the nation's capital—it's found
throughout the country, as meaningful policymaking gets put on
hold for arguing with one another and combating misinformation.
But having traveled coast to coast and beyond, I don't believe this
current reality must dictate our future. Americans at our core are
more similar than different. A firefighter in New Jersey loves his

family just as fiercely as a teacher in Chicago loves hers. An artist in Los Angeles and a ranch hand in Texas both enjoy a good night out with friends.

What makes us human remains the same, and throughout our country's history we have shown we can set aside our differences to come together in times of need, show compassion toward one another, and overcome any tribulation. My grandfathers, members of the Greatest Generation, answered the call to fight tyranny and end genocide in World War II. In my lifetime, I remember the solidarity and camaraderie following September 11, 2001; we were gentler with one another and everyone was wearing I Love NY T-shirts and hanging American flags from their windows. We were collectively wounded, but we weren't broken. We were united. This is the resiliency that makes me proud to be American.

I am in love with the United States of America. It is a place of dreams, the home of both rugged individualism and the deepest bonds of community. It is also an ancient land that has borne some of the wildest creatures, oldest living things, and most spectacular scenery. It is home to Native peoples who know it by different names and know how to live in harmony with the earth. Traveling throughout our country and learning about it is like meeting someone new—someone you grow to love and admire despite their quirks, who teaches you a great deal and encourages you to be the best version of yourself. When home provides to you in this way, you want to protect and preserve it. That's the United States to me, and I'm so grateful I've gotten to know it.

I got to know **Alabama** through a downpour. I've spent a lot of time on the Gulf Coast—growing up, I'd visit Southwest Florida every winter or spring with my parents to see my grandpa—and afternoon showers are hardly surprising. So when I arrived in Alabama around 2 p.m. one day, the deluge brought sweet, albeit brief, relief from the humidity.

Alabama and its neighbor **Mississippi** are two of the few states that aren't getting warmer with climate change. They're not getting drier, either. In fact, the states' normal rainfall is changing to heavier downpours, flooding communities and not absorbing into oversaturated soil. Paired with the intense humidity of the region, this doesn't bode well for crop cycles, a threat expected across many states, including their neighbor to the east.

Next door in **Georgia**, one of many states with an unjust history, having built itself on the backs of slaves and the cotton industry, now finds its agribusiness at this confluence of climates, where hurricanes, wildfires, and tornadoes intermingle. A pecan farmer in Albany, for example, lost 5,000 trees to Hurricane Michael in 2018. The following year, he lost even more to tornadoes.[1] When pecan trees take up to 15 years to produce fruit, losing this many can put a farm out of business and end the farmer's livelihood.

In other crop-yielding states like **Iowa**, **Missouri**, **Nebraska**, and **Oklahoma**, seasons are shifting, and farmers can't predict when to plant their crops or when to harvest them. If the timing isn't just right, seeds can wash away in heavy rains or fruit blossoms may freeze due to seasonally late cold snaps. Warmer temperatures invite pests and disease, and extreme weather events can wipe out an entire season's worth of work.

During my visit to **Kansas** in 2018, I enjoyed traveling between towns and stopping in to find cozy coffee shops, bookstores, and breweries. Although Kansas is considered a "flyover state" by many—often an unfair characterization suggesting a state's value is that it should be flown over when getting from one side of the country to the other—I was particularly excited to see open road and endless grassland, where the earth meets the sky. It's what I envision The Lumineers are describing in their song "Angela."

As I cruised along the rolling terrain, imagining I was Russell Crowe in *Gladiator* as he walks through his wheat fields, clear blue skies turned quickly to dark clouds with winds bending the sparse tall trees. I rushed into a nearby hotel and blurted out, "I'm not from around here. Should I be worried? My dog's in the car!" The kind concierge nonchalantly remarked that it was just a passing storm. Though relieved, I thought about the constant stress on farmers if climate change turns more passing storms into tornadoes.

It's the unpredictability that's problematic for crops—when 44.2 million people already face food insecurity in the United States, inconsistent and inadequate food supply will drive up prices, a reality millions of families simply cannot handle.[2] This played out in 2022 when food costs rose by a staggering 11.4 percent—due in part to drought conditions across the United States—marking the largest increase in food prices since 1979.[3] When weekly groceries cost hundreds of dollars more than a few years ago, families may opt for less food or less healthy food—which is often cheaper—which perpetuates the cycle of hunger. What's more, the rates of hunger double for Black and Latino households compared to white ones.

Elsewhere in the South, heat stress demonstrates the dichotomy of how climate change hits historically underrepresented and overburdened communities considerably harder than white and affluent communities. According to the Brookings Institution, Black and Latino households throughout the United States are less likely to have air-conditioning in the home due to income inequality and the insidious historical practice of redlining, which removed or withheld critical investment—in this case AC installation, shade trees, and green spaces—from poor and minority neighborhoods.

The Carolinas' summers have always been defined by heat and humidity. My first camping experience in **South Carolina** took place late one July along the coast, and even with an ocean breeze, I had to sleep outside of my sleeping bag without a rain fly on the tent. I'm one of those people who can't tolerate the heat when sleeping, but I also need to be covered regardless of temperature—I have some childhood sense the sheets will protect me from monsters. As I tossed and turned, uncomfortable and exposed, I wondered how people—14 million U.S. households, in fact—cope without air-conditioning. With rising temperatures, the heat is getting deadly, killing more than 600 people each year and sending nearly 120,000 more to the emergency room.[4, 5] For families already struggling to put food on the table, a new costly problem arises: how to afford air-conditioning to find relief from extreme heat. When a few utility companies run monopoly-like operations on the energy grid, they can set rates at unaffordable levels, leaving overburdened communities to suffer the worst of changing conditions.

Fortunately, community-owned solar solutions are growing. One company in **North Carolina**, EnerWealth Solutions, is partnering with rural communities to create locally owned electricity, which is making energy more reliable, sustainable, and importantly, affordable. The company saw opportunity in the state's growing solar industry, ranked third in the country in 2023, and has been advocating for better policy planning to ensure the clean energy transition is equitable.[6]

Revitalizing the grid isn't unique to one region of the country. One of **Texas**'s needs in the face of climate change is retrofitting its electric grid, which is nearly entirely independent from the rest of the United States. At first blush, this autonomy has served the state well, avoiding federal regulation and utilizing its abundance of fuel resources to keep the power on. Previously, when the state experienced outages or high demand, it could rely on its massive size, pulling energy resources from elsewhere throughout the state to pick up slack. This changed when unprecedented winter storms froze power plants across the state in 2021 and the sweeping outages led to shortages in food, water, and heat for millions. The disaster was a perfect but preventable storm: power plant operators failed to insulate facilities from prolonged cold, not deeming the investment worth the cost. By the time the power came back, that cost was 246 people—parents, children, and elderly—who lost their lives.[7]

Despite the record-setting low temperatures in winter, Texas is still one of the hottest states in the country, now experiencing this extreme pendulum swing of seasons. And it's not alone. Across the border in **New Mexico**, the state is likely to see increased extreme weather events, like infrequent deluges of rainfall. Unfortunately, in a place that depends on steady snowpack and upriver water sources, this kind of precipitation, brief and infrequent, won't help when facing increased and extended drought. As temperatures warm, snowpack is melting and rivers are drying up, so the unreliable precipitation isn't enough to quench diminishing aquifers.

The American Southwest really awakens my soul. It sings in ancient melody, paints with some of the most incredible hues, and carries wisdom in its wind. I'm not exaggerating for the sake of good writing. If you haven't been, go visit and allow yourself to simply exist: if you are patient and listen carefully, you'll see what I mean.

Here, the Colorado River Watershed, one of the most complex and important water systems in the world, supports more than 40 million people across seven states, and it's drying up. Since 2000, the Southwest has been experiencing the worst megadrought in 1,200 years.[8] As reservoirs fall to record lows, each state is staking its claim to water rights, much of which is being dictated by the needs of agriculture, which often leaves underrepresented, specifically Indigenous, people out of the conversation.

In my travels through **Arizona**, I was blown away by the number of almond farms I saw. Almond trees are notoriously water-intensive, which got me thinking: in this arid region, how much land, and subsequently water, is being allotted to crops that could be usurping the area's most precious resource? I found that a whopping 74 percent of the state's water use is gulped up by agriculture, including water-intensive crops like almonds and alfalfa.[9] The latter, along with hays for cattle feed, need more than half of the Colorado River water designated for irrigated agriculture; meanwhile, those almonds, shows one study, have a total water footprint nearly triple that of the next neediest thirsty crop.[10, 11] In Arizona (and elsewhere), the state constitution permits anyone with the money to buy land, input whatever commodity they choose, and drill for water to sustain it. Here, profit-hungry business folk are buying land upriver of communities whose water faucets are already reduced to a trickle. When it comes to crops like almonds, the incentive lies in the economic value. Money today is apparently worth water scarcity tomorrow.

The water of the West isn't just for drinking or irrigating. In **Nevada**, the Hoover Dam provides electricity to 1.3 million people, but the megadrought, which is lowering Lake Mead's water levels, has already cut power production by half.[12] If the dam ceases to be a reliable source of power, energy will be replaced with more expensive, less clean alternatives.

Even though the West stands at the foreboding edge of water crisis, it's experiencing population booms throughout. And I was almost one of the migrators. **Utah** stole my heart when a trip to visit all of the state's national parks convinced me I needed to live there. Arches and Zion top most visitors' must-see lists, but Capitol Reef, home of some of the best pies in America, really impressed me with its towering rock faces of auburn red and burnt orange against dark blue skies. Since that initial trip to Utah, I've returned several times to explore both the wilderness and real estate. During one visit, my dog, Argos, and I hiked, paddled, and camped—the kind of adventure that, to me, exemplifies a version of "life elevated," one of Utah's mottos conveying both the imposing rock and mountain landscapes as well as the live-every-moment-to-its-fullest mentality. Argos was still a pup at the time, just over a year old: bouncy with a healthy zest for life. On one canyon hike we trekked across streams, under overhangs, and through pockets of cotton-wood forests. As we scrambled up one boulder, Argos lost traction, sliding backward off the edge. I quickly grabbed his harness and yanked him up. It might've only been about five feet off the ground, but I think it was the first time he experienced fear, because once on stable ground, he gave me a slew of sloppy kisses as if to say, "Thanks! That was a close one!"

Ultimately we decided not to move out there, and perhaps for good reason. Less annual snowpack, combined with a population boom up north (thanks to general affordability), is causing the Wasatch Front to run out of water. The popular region, from Brigham City through Salt Lake City down to Provo, gets its water from three rivers east of the capital that are drying up. What's more is the Great Salt Lake is also drying up, and its cracked waterbed is releasing arsenic, literally poisoning the air. But there's good news here: state lawmakers on both sides of the aisle agree that urgent action is needed.

Political will, a term referring to the earnest action and com-mitment to compromise of elected leaders, is what we need the most to address the climate crisis. In **Vermont**, for example, state agencies began incorporating climate considerations into statewide plans in 2005, acknowledging that climate change would affect the state's wildlife, and in 2008 with the Agency of Transportation's Climate Action Plan. Then in 2012, the state created a Climate Cabinet to coordinate across state agencies to both reduce emissions and prepare for the impacts of climate change. More of this, please.

Nearby in **Massachusetts**, Boston is leading by example with climate resilience guidelines for infrastructure, coastal flooding, and housing, with each neighborhood constructing its own plan; the city even has a "Heat Plan" to help prepare residents for the intense heat waves expected in the coming years. In 2024, the city established an Office of Climate Resilience to build on and expand the work of a government initiative known as Climate Ready Boston—a key example of how local politics can overcome partisanship to make immense positive impact on our collective path forward.

Broadly, New England is seeing more pronounced storms and abbreviated winters. States like **Connecticut** and **Rhode Island** expect more hurricanes to travel up the coast, which will require them to shore up for flooding; however, this comes with the possibility that hardening coastlines—that is, developing concrete seawalls or bulkheads—will decrease water quality and increase erosion. Along the eastern seaboard, other states previously unfamiliar with hurricanes are responding similarly.

In 2012, Superstorm Sandy devastated the Jersey Shore. As stronger storms pummel the coast, hardened coastlines like the heavily developed beaches in **New Jersey** lose their natural ability to protect against strong waves and winds. "Jersey Strong" became an anthem for rebuilding after the storm. But part of our resilience requires working *with* the land, not just building on top of it. Don't get me wrong, having lived in Jersey for seven years and as a childhood visitor to its beaches, I associate specific homes, restaurants, and amusement parks with the Shore—some things just go hand in hand with one another. But the harsh new reality is that the state may need to start rebuilding further inland. In its southern neighbor **Delaware**, the second smallest state in our nation, the option to move inland simply doesn't exist, illustrating just one pocket of climate refugees the United States will see if we don't act.

More than a decade after Superstorm Sandy hit New York City, the city's subway system remains extremely vulnerable to flooding. I remember the night Sandy hit—I was sitting in my 11th floor apartment overlooking Riverside Park, the Hudson River, and beyond, New Jersey. Hours into screaming winds and angry rain, New Jersey disappeared—the power had gone out. As I stared into an eerie darkness of one of the country's most densely populated suburbs, south of Wall Street the South Ferry subway station was filling with 15 million gallons of saltwater.[13] It didn't reopen for another five years, as the Metropolitan Transportation Authority worked to create a resilient station that would be prepared for "the next storm." Years after that single station's renovation, the city faces a much bigger problem: in just the first few months of 2024, 200 subway stations flooded during major storms.[14]

In upstate **New York**, local biodiversity is shifting. Referring to the variety of life on earth, biodiversity is responsible for supporting healthy ecosystems, which in turn hold answers to climate change. In New York, for example, forests, marshes, and swamps play an integral role as buffers to strong winds and flooding. As winters become milder and summers hotter, plants, insects, and even some mammals that used to live further south are expanding into new territory, creating unanticipated competition for native species. Agricultural pests that typically died off in winter are sticking around longer. Pests paired with hotter summers are hurting the state's dairy industry; specifically, cows are getting sick and feeling heat stress.

A good friend of mine who splits her time between Southern California and Central America often invites me to come visit any time I'm in search of a getaway. She immediately follows up her offer with a chuckle and, "But I know you hate the heat." While I *can* tolerate the heat, it's the humidity that makes me downright ornery, which makes me sympathetic for the people in the Midwest, in states like **Minnesota**, **Wisconsin**, **Illinois**, and **Indiana**—places that know humid summers but are starting to see life-threatening temperatures and in frequency never known before. City dwellers experience the urban heat island effect—where developed areas experience higher temperatures due to their absorption of heat—while outdoor laborers are rarely given breaks during their workday, illuminating the need for increased green spaces and green roofs in cities, and improved regulations to protect the people working labor-intensive jobs.

Argos and I road-tripped out to these states in the summertime one year, and there was no shortage of activities within state parks or festivals in cities. As is our habit, we hit the trails one day, clambering rigorously along a lakeside loop with modest elevation gain. Argos is a mountain dog, so I wasn't concerned about his ability to keep up, but with the temperature in the 80s, I cut the loop short in case he got too hot. By the end of the hike we were both tuckered out, but I could tell something wasn't right with him. Even after jumping into the lake and cooling off in air-conditioning, he wasn't drinking water. Sure enough, when I got him to an emergency vet, I found out he was experiencing heat exhaustion. In all our hikes since, I've taken measures to avoid encountering these combined conditions again. The way we all plan our vacations or weekend outings will shift in the face of climate change, yes, but what about the wild creatures that aren't responsible for climate change? I think about them a lot, especially in places that are seeing increased natural disaster, like **California**, **Oregon**, and **Washington** with wildfires.

These states are among the most progressive and proactive when it comes to climate policy. In fact, California, with support from the federal government and a conservation group called Save the Redwoods League, repatriated 125 acres of culturally important land to the Yurok people, the original stewards of this land parcel. In this first-of-its-kind agreement, the Yurok will take on managing the land, resuming ancient practices that will protect the immensely important coastal redwoods.[15]

Native American elders across tribes find much of North America unrecognizable today. In my day job, my team works with tribes to restore habitats and species to their historic ranges. In conversations with representatives of the Blackfeet and Sicangu

Lakota Nations, for example, I've learned compelling histories of bison—their relative—and the animal's role in songs and ceremonies; however, these traditions have lain dormant for generations. Elsewhere, our Hopi and Zuni friends have described to my team the way beavers long ago helped to retain moisture along tributaries of the Rio Grande in a region where reliable, consistent water flow is critical. Unfortunately in both instances, and countless others, so much has been lost due to colonization and subsequent development and human encroachment. Add climate change to the mix, with warmer rivers and oceans, extreme drought, devastating wildfires, and ravaging hurricanes, and the earth will become inhospitable. Imagining places like the Pacific Northwest, Great Plains, or Southwest as bare and brown—with no orca whales, no bison or beavers, no wolves, pinyon jays, or pond turtles—is not a future I want to tempt.

It doesn't seem fair to lump a lot of states together when describing the effects climate change will have on them—I've learned from my travels that each state beams with pride over its individuality. But climate change doesn't care about arbitrary state lines, and a lot of us are going to feel similar impacts as our neighbors. In this way, it's critical we have federal leadership on climate action in addition to the substantial policy and sector-specific implementation and enforcement needed from states.

Unfortunately, according to the Georgetown Climate Center, as of 2024, 31 states have not finalized a state-led climate adaptation plan. While many of those states do have sector-specific or agency-led plans, and/or locally driven plans or regional collaborations with other states, some had taken no action at all. **Arkansas**, **North Dakota**, **South Dakota**, **West Virginia**, and **Wyoming** have ignored the call to act. At play here, say some social scientists, is the growing populist movement—the anti-e stablishment policymakers and pundits who claim problems like the higher cost of living are the result of elitist and green policies. This rhetoric stokes the concerns of the average American—putting food on the table or meeting healthcare needs—and creates a scapegoat. What's more worrying is the fact that this divisiveness is also fueling a vehement skepticism toward experts. Nobody likes to feel like they're being talked down to, so when scientists try to explain climate change and its human causes, it gets complicated (science has a knack of doing that, which is probably why I never liked chemistry class), and when something is beyond comprehension, most people's reaction is not to investigate further. While that's a normal response, I'd argue that this aversion is exacerbated by the plague that is social media—how it feeds us siloed information and takes away our critical thinking skills, but that's a story for another book. So when a populist can simplify a complicated issue by creating a villain, that's an easier narrative to swallow. If I were a gambling woman, I'd wager these populists are largely motivated by the money snuck into their back pockets by the industries making a profit by maintaining business as usual. If your blood is boiling right now, take a deep breath. The single best way to meet skepticism and divisiveness is with compassion. Change is scary, whether it's being thrust upon us or we're making that choice. Putting ourselves into someone else's shoes creates empathy and harkens to that gentler, united nature Americans find in times of need. And we do need it right now.

States will undoubtedly require the support of others. **Louisiana** and territory **Puerto Rico** are continuously battered by hurricanes. While the Bayou State sits on a relatively flat coastal plain, *isla del encanto* is just that—an island. As storms increase in severity and frequency, eroding away shorelines, and rising seas creep into communities, these two regions have been among the first to produce climate refugees fleeing the ocean. **Michigan** might hold opportunity and answer. Though the state is getting hotter and wetter, scientists project the impacts of climate change may hit the state with less intensity than elsewhere because of its geographic location.

A lot of Americans find it hard to visualize climate refugees within our own country; it's easier to think that these issues are not connected to our own immediate circles, that the problems are far away and someone else's. And it *does* feel that way—until suddenly it doesn't. In 2023, Hurricane Ian decimated Pine Island, **Florida**—the island my family has been calling home for over 40 years. When connections were being drawn between climate change and the storm, the response from some was that people shouldn't live on a tiny island susceptible to these impacts. That's when I got angry. This is a quiet fishermen's island, and the extent of residents' impact on climate change only ranges from a few miles offshore to the waterfront restaurant in town that's serving the crab and catfish they caught earlier in the day. When this has been their modest livelihood for generations, their lives are not so easily shifted. They can't just pick up and leave.

Those who are among the least responsible for what's happening to our planet are often the ones most impacted. This phenomenon is referred to as climate injustice, and communities across the country are being put into similar positions as Pine Island. Overburdened communities in **Washington D.C.** are uniquely at risk because they continue to combat the historical inequities of redlining while having no voice in the federal government. More people live in the District of Columbia than the entire state of Wyoming, yet our nation's capital has no voting power in the halls of Congress because it's not a state. For the city to craft its own policies, it must jump through hoops, which delays action for heat-stressed and flood-prone neighborhoods that did nothing to cause the climate crisis and whose residents are simply trying earn a living and survive.

When livelihoods are threatened, it doesn't just take a toll on family pocketbooks—it impacts mental health as well. In **Ohio**, farmers in rural communities are facing near-record debt, declaring bankruptcy, and selling off their farms due to emerging uncertainty caused by climate change and further amplified by tariffs and bailouts. Between 2014 and 2018, 450 farmers died by suicide in the American Midwest.[16]

To the south in **Kentucky** and **Tennessee**, more people are being displaced. In December 2021, tornadoes ripped through western Kentucky, a state not accustomed to the storms, destroying more than 500 homes.[17] In Tennessee, 560 landslides occurred in Nashville in May 2010 due to unprecedented flooding, which triggered statewide landslide research.[18] Despite repeated efforts by state agencies and state lawmakers on both sides of the aisle, the state has not addressed the increasing risk of floods and landslides.

Alaska and **Hawai'i** are also coming to know displacement intimately. Alaska faces eroding shores due to thawing permafrost and shrinking glaciers, in addition to insect outbreaks and wild-fires. Here, erosion takes on immensely acute meaning. Villages like Newtok and Shishmaref are disappearing. The Native people who have lived here, subsistence-fishing in these specific places for thousands of years, are watching their homes fall into the sea as hundreds of feet of shoreline give in to the wrath of single storms. Similarly in Hawai'i, rising seas could reclaim the volcanic archipelago. Some of those islands are home to the last remaining populations of species of seal, albatross, and songbirds. An island in the tropics synonymous with lush vegetation, Hawai'i doesn't seem like a good fit for wildfires, but with average rainfall declining since 1990, up to 31 percent in some places, the Aloha state has become brittle. In the devastating fires that destroyed historical Lahaina on Maui in 2023, the U.S. Drought Monitor reported that 36 percent of Maui County was in moderate to severe drought. While the cause of the fires was unrelated to climate change, the impact was far more catastrophic because of it.[19]

These states have remarkably strong identities inextricably linked with their natural landscapes. Elsewhere, other states' identities are threatened as snowpack melts and winter precipitation decreases, threatening to take away the recreation that holds them together culturally and economically. **Idaho**, **Montana**, **Colorado**, and **New Hampshire** are getting warmer, winters are getting shorter, and the powder is turning to slush. When I moved to **Maine** in 2019, I was eager to experience up to six months of snow. My best friend even bought me snowshoes as a welcome gift. In Vacationland, home of "the way life should be" state motto, I was shocked that during the two winters I lived there, I didn't break out my snowshoes once. The Gulf of Maine is warming faster than 98 percent of the world's oceans, primarily due to global warming as it impacts ocean currents.

Every summer, I have the privilege to work off the coast of Maine alongside preeminent seabird biologists, and I've seen how the hotter ocean is affecting fish, seabirds, seals, and even sharks, as well as the people who interact with the Gulf. A changing ocean habitat changes the food availability throughout the food chain. When Atlantic puffins must fly farther to find food, they're away from home longer, leaving hungry chicks to risk starvation. What's even more heartbreaking is that when puffin parents can't find the fish necessary for pufflings, they'll come home with a substitute, and sometimes that substitute is too big for a tiny chick to swallow. Again, starvation. The same could happen to our own food sources. The lobster fishery is the state's primary export, and trust me, you don't want to tell those hardy folks they can't go lobster fishing anymore.

Another state I've called home is **Virginia**. In 2020, the governor signed a landmark climate package into law and joined 10 other states in the Regional Greenhouse Gas Initiative to jointly address climate change. In 2024, the new governor approved removing the state from the regional initiative, recommitting to his own energy plan that would repeal the state's clean car standard and loosen other environmental permitting requirements. While environmental groups have filed suit to force the state to reenter the regional initiative, the situation in Virginia paints a clear picture that who you vote for matters.

Next door in **Maryland**, the state's farmlands produce a lot of nutrient pollution, which—as runoff into waterways—can cause what's known as "dead zones." These zones suck oxygen out of the water, killing much of the life that lives below the surface. When this runoff combines with warm water—which is increasing in temperature and duration throughout the year—the dead zones are likely to become more prevalent and pronounced. Living so close to Maryland in both Washington D.C. and Virginia, I see the fight my friends are entrenched in, advocating for better policy and demanding that industry be held accountable.

While I've been fortunate to call many states home, there is one that means more than all the others. When I think of **Pennsylvania**, I think of my backyard as a kid: the bright greens of summertime and the rural-suburban adventures I'd take with my friends. I grew up playing in the Yellow Breeches Creek, jumping off 30-foot cliffs into cool water. In the fall, I'd watch the brilliant colors of autumn settle in as gentle fog would rise up from the creek, and Canada geese would stop on their way south. Winter blew in with soft snow and my dad would build igloos for me. Christmases were often white. Then spring's renewal brought the smell of pear blossoms and the return of geese. Time was punctuated by the different seasons.

As I've gotten older, I've seen more annual Turkey Trots in tank tops and fewer white Christmases. The state is getting warmer and wetter, including more flash flooding, which can carry contaminated water into neighborhoods. I don't want to lose Pennsylvania. It's this home, and every other, that drives me to act.

What You Can Do

When I was about 10 years old, I would watch a kids' program on PBS called *Kratts' Creatures*. Four o'clock became my favorite time of the day, because the Kratt brothers would teach me something new about animals. One day, they introduced the Tasmanian tiger, or thylacine. It was a marsupial in Australia that looked like a dog with an elongated snout and stripes on its back. That day, I learned about extinction. That day, I decided I wanted to prevent extinction from happening to any other animal.

Years later in eighth grade, I was sitting in Mrs. Weltmer's English class when she leaned in to tell us something important: the Twin Towers in New York City had been struck by planes, and we'd be going home shortly. That day, I learned about the world. That day, I decided I wanted to save it.

My life has twisted and turned in ways I didn't expect when I was 10 or in eighth grade. I am still constantly thinking about animals and how to save the world, though. I know what motivates me, and each day I wake up pursuing what brings me joy and leaves me fulfilled. That's my wish for you.

The world doesn't need any one of us to take on the sole responsibility of saving it (note to self). It needs us to find our passions and dig in. So when you're ready, here's how to get started.

Learn About Something

You don't need to know everything about everything, or even *a little* about everything. Just *something*. Find what resonates with you and become the expert among your friends and family. Pick up another book like this one, sign up for newsletters, and follow accounts and outlets that will inform you with credible, unbiased information. Share what you've learned. Find groups that are active around the issue and support them by volunteering or donating. Friends often ask me how best to discern a group that's doing good work from one that's not. There's no one-size-fits-all answer, but typically, local groups have direct impact on their communities, while large nonprofits can mobilize and generate awareness. The biggest takeaway is to do your research and stay curious.

Consume Wisely

Every single thing we purchase has a backstory, and with enough digging, you might find that that origin story is often villainous. Rainforests are decimated, oceans are overfished, and waterways are poisoned with waste from chemical factories. Rethinking our habitual consumption is a way to fight back. *Do I need this?* is a question I ask myself often. I treat myself plenty, don't get me wrong, but those treats have definitely evolved the more I learn about sourcing and production. Generally, buying local and less, choosing natural fiber textiles, opting for secondhand, asking for the source of a product, and being aware of greenwashing—a term referring to false advertising companies will use to give the impression they're committed to sustainability or positive environmental impact—are great ways to consume more wisely.

Then there's mass monoculture—that is, industrial scale agriculture of one crop or product that clear-cuts and decimates habitats and often forcibly ousts Indigenous peoples from their land. Commodities like beef, soy, palm oil, and timber are extremely taxing on the environment, notwithstanding the losses incurred by local biodiversity and indigenous communities. Reducing or eliminating consumption of these commodities are some of the biggest positive impacts we can have on the climate. Look at ingredient labels, ask where products were sourced, then make an informed selection.

What happens to goods after we consume them impacts the planet significantly as well. The majority of plastics cannot actually be recycled, for example, and the dark reality of the fashion industry is that it's exploitative and destructive. Choose reusable items for longer-term use, hang on to clothing items (they'll come back into fashion), and choose package-free or bulk items.

In addition to where we spend our money, where we keep our money matters too. Many banks in the United States and globally are still funding the fossil fuel industry despite adopting policies designed to help avert climate catastrophe. If your bank is among them, take your money elsewhere.

Make Space for Species

Indigenous cultures know well that sharing the planet with all its inhabitants enables the natural balance needed for life as we know it. Keep in mind that rich biodiversity is a natural defense against climate change, so protecting our landscapes and creatures is climate action. In the United States, 60 percent of land is privately owned, so if you have a yard, create a wildlife habitat by providing native plants as food and shelter. Avoid using pesticides that kill pollinators like bees, who are responsible for nearly one in every three bites of food. Leave fallen leaves or dying trees (if it's safe to do so), which provide a home to wintering insects and help to create nutrient-rich soil.

City dwellers have a part to play as well; on anything from balcony spaces to green roofs, plant native species to serve the local pollinators. If neither space exists, ask building management to consider creating a rooftop or community garden. If nothing else, consider joining tree-planting initiatives or starting your own. Not only will the birds and bees thank you, but it'll cool the space, providing reprieve from increasing temperatures.

Eat Smart

The foods we eat and the way they're produced have an outsized impact on the planet, both on the climate and what's left of arable land. Crop and livestock production are the main sources of water pollution by nitrates, phosphates, and pesticides, and both wipe out suitable habitat for native species, plant and animal. Changing food choices can have sweeping impacts on the planet's species.

Eating seasonally, choosing local over imported foods, and choosing regenerative foods that minimize impact to local ecosystems and support local communities are among the best choices.

Going vegetarian or vegan also drastically decreases individual climate impact. Collectively, diet shifts and smarter food choices can combat one of the largest sectors of human-caused climate change.

Use Your Voice

Vote for candidates who prioritize the future of our planet and research which ones are getting campaign contributions from questionable sources—then vote them out! Call elected officials or schedule meetings with them to ask what actions they're taking to address climate change. Attend town halls. Participate in peaceful demonstrations, marches, and protests. Use your voice wherever you are. The activities of an office, group, business, or multinational all have impact. If we don't speak up where we are, we won't see change.

There is no shortage of actions we can take in the fight against climate change, and the suggestions provided in these pages are hardly prescriptive. What matters is that we understand we do not own this planet—we borrow it from our children, and they share it with an abundance of magnificent life, from cortinarius mushrooms and spotted salamanders to gray wolves and bristlecone pine trees. The earth is what we all have in common, our existence having emerged from the wilds, not big cities. Here in the United States, we find ourselves divided, forgetting these commonalities and forgetting that we're in this together. Consider this your reminder. Our future is asking us to approach with respect and compassion, urgency and will. I believe we can respond in kind—don't you?

Additional Resources

Books

All We Can Save: Truth, Courage, and Solutions for the Climate Crisis edited by Ayana Elizabeth Johnson and Katharine K. Wilkinson

Braiding Sweetgrass by Robin Wall Kimmerer

Dirt Road Revival: How to Rebuild Rural Politics and Why Our Future Depends On It by Chloe Maxmin and Canyon Woodward

Emergent Strategy by Adrienne Maree Brown

How to Go (Almost) Zero Waste by Rebecca Grace Andrews

On Digital Advocacy: Saving the Planet While Preserving Our Humanity by Katie Boué

Saving Us: A Climate Scientist's Case for Hope and Healing in a Divided World by Katharine Hayhoe

The Octopus in the Parking Garage: A Call for Climate Resilience by Rob Verchick

Podcasts

Agents of Change in Environmental Justice

America Adapts: The Climate Change Podcast

Climate One

The Wild

Documentaries

Farming While Black

Kiss the Ground

The Grab

The Human Element

Check out the Environmental Film Festival in the Nation's Capital website for hundreds of films available online now. Visit dceff.org.

Social Media

@ClimateReality

@ClimateGenOrg

@Grist

@UNClimateChange

State Governors' Contact Information

nga.org/governors

Acknowledgments

Though this book may be short, the list of those who helped it come to light is long. Thank you to:

The team at Fulcrum Books for believing in this idea and guiding me through drafts and edits, Alyse Knorr for her beautiful insight and suggestions to make this book the best version of itself.

Scott Weidensaul and Lucy Sherriff for giving this book a chance and being among the first to review it! Rob Verchick for the creative conversation and encouragement, Stevan Knapp for reading early versions of the haiku and providing wonderfully thoughtful feedback, Charlotte Aubrey for her keen insight as an eight-year-old.

Everyone who has—whether by guestroom, couch, meal, or otherwise—indulged my cross-country travel, including but not limited to Jared Messinger—who convinced me there was so much of this country worth seeing—Megan and Chris Paone, Jean and Paul Colon, Rusty Stauder, Alana Miller and Brittney Britt, Kelsie and Ed DeFrancia and Sharon Brussell, Claire Van Zuiden and Kevin Hartsoch, Alex Bogdan, Chris White, Terry Dewane, Tom Dewane, Amie Boswell, Whitney Clark, Gabrielle Benoit, Jessica Bailey Wyatt, Tess Holman, Dan Robicheaux, Frankie Heller, Nick Popoli, Frank Reig and Mirjam Grunenfelder, Alli Roddy, James Olszewski, Katie Jurek, Alexis Howell, Courtney Whistler, Kelly Allred.

The team at the Center for Progressive Reform for teaching me about ways to address climate change that go beyond just the talking points.

The team at Defenders of Wildlife for being eager cheerleaders and advisors on this project.

Kelly Armijo, Kayla Nielsen, Jess Shuman for your enduring support, joy, and love. Your adventuring, ambitious kindred spirits are the kind that everyone should have in their corner cheering them on.

Adam DiNuovo, surely my big brother from another lifetime. Your support and guidance are greater than any words could convey.

Mom, Dad, and Mollie. Thank you for being. I love you more than two universes and five really big dinosaurs.

Endnotes

1   Shane Keating, et al., "Damages On Pecan Farms After Hurricane Michael," Georgia Public Broadcasting, June 26, 2019, http://stories.georgiaclimateproject. org/pecan-farmer

2   Matthew P. Rabbit, et al., "Household Food Security in the United States in 2022," *Economic Research Service* 325 (October 2023): 10, https://www.ers. usda.gov/webdocs/publications/ 107703/err-325.pdf?v=7814.4

3   Sam Stone, "Grocery Price News Is All Over the Place. What's Really Happening?" *Bon Appetit*, June 20, 2023, https://www.bonappetit.com/story/ 2023-grocery-prices

4   Ambarish Vaidyanathan, PhD, et al., "Heat-Related Emergency Department Visits—United States, May–September 2023" *Morbidity and Mortality Weekly Report* 73 (April 18, 2024): 324–329. DOI: https://www.cdc.gov/mmwr/volumes/73/wr/mm7315a1.htm

5   Rebecca Mann and Jenny Schuetz, "As Extreme Heat Grips the Globe, Access to Air Conditioning Is an Urgent Public Health Issue," Brookings Institution, July 25, 2022, https://www.brookings.edu/articles/as-extreme-heat-grips-the-globe-access-to-air-conditioning-is-an-urgent-public-health-issue/

6   Matt Chester, "10 States Leading Solar Installation in 2023," EcoWatch, February 22, 2023, https://www.ecowatch.com/solar/states-leading-solar-energy-installation

7   "February 2021 Winter Storm-Related Deaths – Texas," December 31, 2023, Texas Health and Human Services, https://www.dshs.texas.gov/sites/default/ files/news/updates/SMOC_FebWinterStorm_MortalitySurvReport_12-30-21.pdf

8   A.P. Williams, et al., "Rapid Intensification of the Emerging Southwestern North American Megadrought in 2020–2021," *Nature Climate Change* 12 (2022): 232–234, https://doi.org/10.1038/s41558-022-01290-z

9   Arizona Department of Water Resources, Conservation, Agriculture, https:// www.azwater.gov/conservation/agriculture

10 B. D. Richter, G. Lamsal, L. Marston, et al., "New Water Accounting Reveals Why the Colorado River No Longer Reaches the Sea," Communications Earth & Environment 5, 134 (2024), https://doi.org/10.1038/s43247-024-01291-0

11 Julian Fulton, Michael Norton, and Fraser Shilling, "Water-Indexed Benefits and Impacts of California Almonds," Science Direct 96 (January 2019): 711–717 https://www.sciencedirect.com/science/article/pii/S1470160X17308592#f0030

12 Rachel Ramirez, "The West's Historic Drought Is Threatening Hydropower at Hoover Dam," CNN, August 16, 2022, https://www.cnn.com/2022/08/16/us/hoover-dam-hydropower-drought-climate/index.html

13 Katherine Creag, "South Ferry Subway Station Reopens 5 Years After Sandy Flooding," NBC 4 New York, June 27, 2017, https://www.nbcnewyork.com/news/local/south-ferry-station-whitehall-street-damaged-floodwater-super-storm-sandy-mta-passengers-reopens/189053/

14 Andrew Siff, "200 NYC Subway Stations Have Flooded in Recent Storms, 22 of Which Need Major Fixes: MTA," NBC 4 New York, January 31, 2024, https://www.nbcnewyork.com/news/local/200-nyc-subway-stations-have-flooded-in-recent-storms-22-of-which-need-major-fixes-mta/5093801/#

15 "Partners to Co-manage Public Access at Future Gateway to Redwood National and State Parks," Save the Redwoods League, March 19, 2024, https://www.savetheredwoods.org/press-releases/historic-agreement-to-return-tribal-land/

16 Katie Wedell, et al., "Midwest Farmers Face a Crisis. Hundreds Are Dying by Suicide," *USAToday*, March 9, 2020, https://www.usatoday.com/in-depth/news/investigations/2020/03/09/ climate-tariffs-debt-and-isolation-drive-some-farmers-suicide/4955865002/#:~:text=But%20U.S.%20farmers%20are%20saddled,the%20burden%20is%20too%20much

17 Joseph Garcia, "Revisiting Western Kentucky One Year After Deadly Torna-does," WHAS11, December 9, 2022, https://www.whas11.com/article/weather/kentucky-tornadoes/western-kentucky-december-2021-tornadoes-mayfield-dawson-springs-bowling-green-severe-weather/417-bd8410e9-1e01-4408-a631-785e4a623247

18 Caroline Eggers, "Landslides, Floods Might Get Mapped in Tennessee Under New Bills," WPLN News, February 21, 2024, https://wpln.org/post/landslides-floods-might-get-mapped-in-tennessee-under-new-bills/

19 Christopher Flavelle and Manuela Andreoni, "How Climate Change Turned Lush Hawaii Into a Tinderbox," *New York Times*, August 10, 2023, https://www.nytimes.com/2023/08/10/climate/hawaii-fires-climate-change.html

About the Author

Maggie Dewane is an author, activist, and explorer who has traveled to all seven continents to understand climate change, conservation, and how both impact people.

Her professional experience spans the U.S. Senate, White House Council on Environmental Quality, and multiple environmental nonprofits, including Defenders of Wildlife. She serves on the board and advisory councils to Birdability and the Environmental Film Festival in the Nation's Capital, and leads an annual weeklong seabird conservation summer camp in Maine with the Audubon Society. Maggie holds a BS from Seton Hall University in diplomacy and international relations and an MPA from Columbia University in environmental science and policy.

Maggie lives with her dog, Argos, and can often be found playing soccer or planning her next adventure.